by Stuart Schwartz and Craig Conley

Content Consultant:
Robert J. Miller, Ph.D.
Associate Professor
Mankato State University

CAPSTONE
HIGH/LOW BOOKS
an imprint of Capstone Press

C A P S T O N E   P R E S S

818 North Willow Street • Mankato, MN 56001
http://www.capstone-press.com

Library of Congress Cataloging-in-Publication Data
Schwartz, Stuart, 1945-
    Working as a team/by Stuart Schwartz and Craig Conley.
    p. cm. -- (Job skills)
    Includes bibliographical references and index.
    Summary: Explains how to function effectively and productively in the workplace
as part of a team.
    ISBN 1-56065-718-9
    1. Teams in the workplace--Juvenile literature. [1. Teams in the workplace.]
I. Conley, Craig, 1965- . II. Title. III. Series: Schwartz, Stuart, 1945- Job skills.
HD66.S39 1998
658.4'036--dc21   97-53220
                                                    CIP
                                                     AC

Photo credits:
All photos by Dede Smith Photography

Table of Contents

Chapter | 1

Teamwork Counts

Employers hire people who work well with others. An employer is a person or company that hires and pays workers. Employers call workers employees.

Employers often call groups of workers teams. Team members work together to reach goals. This is called teamwork. For example, police officers work together to stop crime. Television crews work together to make movies and shows.

Good team members need special skills. They know how to listen and share ideas. They respect the rights of others. They work well with people who are different from them. Good team members also know their employer's goals. They know how they can help reach these goals.

Workers can learn to become good team members by practicing needed skills. They can help their employers by being good team members.

Employers hire people who work well with others.

Chapter 2

Teamwork and Success

Teamwork helps people succeed. Each member of a team contributes something. Contribute means offering help to a group or organization.

For example, food servers try to serve customers well. A customer is a person who buys goods or services. Servers who help each other can serve customers better. Team members can help clean up if one server spills something. Another server may serve extra customers if one server is busy.

Workers may have different jobs on a team. But they all share the same goal. Each member helps the team reach its goal.

Teamwork helps everyone succeed. Employers succeed because teams help them reach their goals. Workers succeed by earning money and keeping their jobs. Customers benefit from better service or better products.

Workers may have different jobs on a team.

Chapter 3

Becoming a Team Member

Workers must earn their place on a team. They must know their jobs. They must work hard. They must also be honest. Team members must be able to trust each other. For example, fire fighters must trust their co-workers to help put out fires.

Becoming a team member does not happen the first day on the job. Workers can get to know each other on breaks. Getting to know each other will make workers better team members.

Members must do their share of the work to be part of a team. Others must do more if some workers do not do their share. The team succeeds when everyone works hard.

Good team members know how their team helps the employer. They understand the team's goals. For example, nurses take care of sick people. They understand how their work helps others. They know their work makes their employer successful. They work to reach their goal so everyone succeeds.

Workers can get to know each other during breaks.

Chapter — 4

Sharing Ideas

Every member of a team is important. Every worker has suggestions to share. A suggestion is an idea. Workers can suggest faster ways to do jobs. They can suggest ways of saving money. They can suggest ways of improving a company's products.

Team members work together to make good suggestions succeed. A house painter might suggest using a different kind of paint. The painter shares the suggestion with the team. The team members talk about the suggestion. They consider whether it will help the team and the employer. They start using the new paint if it will help the team and the employer. Using the new paint results in better painting.

Workers at a shoe store might want to sell more shoes. One team member suggests a special sale. The other team members discuss the idea. They decide to try it. The whole team works together to make the sale a success.

Every worker has suggestions to share.

Chapter 5

Listening

Team members listen to each other. They give each person a chance to talk. Team members let each other finish speaking. They consider everyone's suggestions.

Good team members show they are interested in other members' suggestions. They look at the speaker. They give their full attention. They show they understand. They might nod their heads or answer the speaker's questions.

Team members discuss each other's ideas. They tell others when they agree. They thank each other for sharing suggestions.

A team that listens well does a better job. For example, construction workers are a team. They build streets and buildings. Good construction workers listen to each other. They listen to suggestions about how to make buildings stronger and safer.

Good team members listen to each other.

Chapter 6

Reaching Goals

All employers have goals. Grocery store owners want to sell food. Hospital managers want to help sick people get well.

Teams of workers have goals, too. Their goals are part of employers' goals.

People who work at schools are team members. One teacher helps students learn to read. Another teacher helps students learn math. Custodians make sure the schools are clean. These workers have different jobs. But they all have the same goal. They want to help students.

Good team members learn about the goals of other team members. They share ideas about how to reach the goals. For example, reading teachers might share suggestions with math teachers. They help each other teach students. This helps the school succeed.

Good team members learn the goals of others.

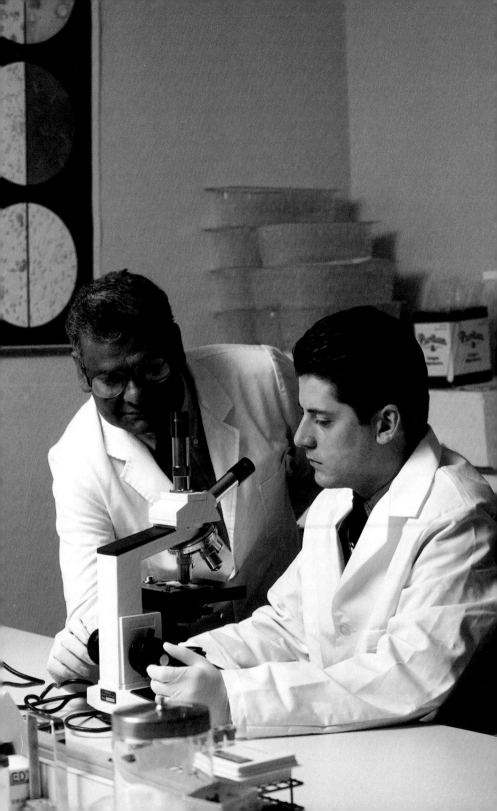

Chapter | 7

Building on Strengths

Each team member has strengths. Each team member has weaknesses. Good teams learn to use the strengths of team members.

Team members learn their strong points in different ways. Supervisors try to help team members see their strengths. A supervisor is a person in charge of workers.

Sometimes team members learn their own strengths. Team members might take turns doing different tasks. Then they might discuss the tasks. They decide who does well at one task. They decide who does well at another.

For example, employees at a restaurant perform many tasks. A restaurant is a place where people pay to eat meals. One team member might be a good cook. Another might be good at serving meals. Another might wash dishes the fastest. Strong teams depend on each member's strengths to reach goals.

Good teams use the strengths of team members.

Chapter 8

Working with Different People

Good team members can work with others who are not like them. They work with people who have different skin colors. They work with people of different ages. They work with both men and women. They work with people of different religions. Team members must get along with others to do a good job.

Good team members know that differences can make a team strong. Different people solve problems in different ways. They can help each other find the best solutions.

All team members can contribute something to the team. Young workers may have a lot of energy. Older workers may have more experience.

Good team members can work with different people.

Chapter 9

Respecting Rights

All workers have the same basic rights. Team members must respect each other's rights. Good team members think about how they want to be treated. They treat others the way they themselves want to be treated.

Workers have the right to share their ideas. They have the right to be treated fairly. They have the right to have a safe workplace.

Most employers have rules that protect workers' rights. Some rules tell how employees should treat each other. These rules may be written or spoken. Good team members know and follow the rules. They show their respect for the rights of others by doing this.

Respecting rights helps the team operate smoothly. It helps team members get along with each other. It can even prevent workplace injuries.

Team members respect each other's rights.

Chapter — 10

Solving Problems

Problems often come up on the job. Good team members must be able to solve their problems. Sometimes team members disagree about how to do this.

Sometimes one worker makes a mistake. Another worker may feel angry. Good team members talk about the problem. Team members say what they think the problem is. They say why they think the problem occurred.

Good team members know how to compromise. Compromise means to reach an agreement. In a compromise, each side gives up something it wants. But each side also gets something it wants.

For example, two custodians might disagree about who should mop the floors. They talk about their choices. They decide to take turns mopping. The custodians have made a good compromise.

Teams must be able to solve their problems.

Chapter — **11**

Being Flexible

Team members must be flexible. They must be willing to adjust to new situations. Sometimes a team's goals change. Sometimes a team member's job changes. Good team members adapt to the change. They work toward new goals. They learn new jobs. They continue being good team members.

Changes can be hard and confusing. Sometimes team members have to work with new people. They must spend time training new workers. Sometimes workers have to learn how to use new machines. Good team members do not give up. They do their best to be flexible.

Team members can help others be flexible. One person might know how to use a new machine. That team member can teach others how to use it.

A store owner might decide to sell a new product. Sales clerks can help each other learn about the product. Teams that are flexible can learn to do many jobs.

Team members can help others be flexible.

Chapter | 12

Teamwork and You

Being a good team member will help you do better work. You can help your team succeed. You can feel proud of reaching goals.

Think of other times when you were a team member. How did you contribute? Your family may be like a team. How do you contribute to your family? You might help teach family members who need help. You might do extra work when needed. You can be a team member at work, too.

You can also think about how good team members act. You can practice listening, sharing, and getting along with others. You can think about your strengths. You can use your strengths to help your team.

Being a good team member takes work. But it is worth the effort. Employers trust workers who are good team members. Teamwork can help your team, your employer, and you.

Being a good team member will help you.

Words to Know

compromise (KOM-pruh-mize)—to reach an agreement

contribute (kuhn-TRIB-yoot)—to offer help to a group or organization

customer (KUHSS-tuh-mur)—a person who buys goods or services

employer (em-PLOI-ur)—a person or company that pays people to work

restaurant (RESS-tuh-rahnt)—a place where people pay to eat meals

suggestion (suhg-JES-chuhn)—an idea about how to do something

supervisor (SOO-pur-vye-zur)—a person in charge of workers

To Learn More

Gartner, Robert. *High Performance Through Teamwork*. New York: Rosen Publishing Group, 1996.

Ludden, LaVerne. *Job Savvy: How to Be a Success at Work*. Indianapolis, Ind.: JIST Works, 1998.

Schwartz, Stuart and Craig Conley. *Communicating with Others*. Mankato, Minn.: Capstone High/Low Books, 1998.

Useful Addresses

Canada WorkInfoNet
Room 2161
Asticou Training Centre
241 Boulevard Cite des Jeunes
Hull, Quebec K1A 0M7
Canada

Employment and Training Administration
200 Constitution Avenue NW
Room N-4700
Washington, DC 20210

U.S. Department of Labor
Office of Public Affairs
200 Constitution Avenue NW
Room S-1032
Washington, DC 20210

Internet Sites

America's Job Bank
http://www.ajb.dni.us

Skills Most in Demand by Employers
http://www.utoronto.ca/career/skills.htm

The Training Information Source
http://www.training-info.com/

Index